Apocalypse Rising

Apocalypse Rising

and other works

J.S. Sutton

To order additional copies of this book, contact:
Xlibris Corporation
0-800-644-6988
www.xlibrispublishing.co.uk
Orders@Xlibrispublishing.co.uk
302232

Contents

Apocalypse Rising

With tired and aching legs he sat down on the steps at Swansea beach. His right forearm bleeding and painful from the bite he suffered at the hands of his dearest friend. He sighed as he viewed the splendour of the sunrise over the hills by Port Talbot, then Neath, then Swansea itself. He shuddered when he heard the moans and groans of the dead, as if the world he came to know over the past week had had a resuscitating breath of life again. By the volume of the groaning he speculated that the dead were far, but not far enough to loiter here for any particular length of time so he made his way down the beach towards mumbles and knab rock where he was certain that, if the tide was in, he would be safe, for a while at least. His appearance left a lot to be desired, unkempt jaw length shaggy hair, thick beard soaked in blood (rarely his own), his clothes caked in mud, sand and blood. "I wonder if any survivors would mistake me for the undead if they saw me" he thought. The smith and western air rifle felt heavy in his blood stained hands, the right breast pocket of his green and black plaid shirt sagged like a branch of weeping willow tree due to the 15 bullets he had left. "Keep one bullet" he thought "I'm never going to let myself become one of those things!". When he got to mumbles pier it seemed deserted but, as the things he experienced up to this point taught him, that was rarely the case. He cocked the rifle and proceeded with extreme caution. Suddenly there was a crash to the right of him, a cat had jumped on a bin causing it to topple over under its weight. Then to the left of him he heard a groan as a dead guy came stumbling out of the amusement arcade, then another came out of the mini ice rink. "Shit!" he cried and he ran between the two towards the steep staircase down to the beach and the causeway of knab rock. As he got down the stairs another four were waiting for him at the bottom so he turned around and, with a practiced hand, dispatched the two that were following him. He then proceeded to cave in the heads of three of the ones that were at the bottom of the stairs with the butt of his rifle, when it came to the fourth he rammed the rifle in its mouth and pulled the trigger causing its skull to blossom like a spring flower. He crossed the causeway to knab rock and climbed to the summit. There was a zombie there as well so he clubbed it with the rifle butt. Across the bay roughly fifty meters away was the knab rock light house. "Should I swim there?" he asked himself. He looked back at the mainland and the pier, more zombies were gathering, attracted by the gunshots no doubt. "Fuck it!" he thought and dived into the sea. In roughly fifteen minutes he reached the lighthouse. As he began climbing the rocky wall that made the mini island's coast he heard a voice over a loud speaker. "Who are you and what do you want?" it said. "I am Jim and I need safety!!" Jim cried back. "Come on up then friend!" the loud speaker replied. As Jim approached the door of the lighthouse it opened to reveal a heavy set man with balding grey hair and a thick grey beard. "Come on!" he said in a thick south welsh accent "hurry up lad!". Jim sprinted into the lighthouse and there was a massive clang as the door was slammed shut and bolted. The heat of the log fire in the corner made Jim's glasses steam up so he took them off and cleaned them on his shirt. When he put them back on again his improved sight was greeted with a beautiful young girl with raven black hair. "Sit yourself down" she said also with a thick south welsh accent "I'll make you a broth and my grandfather will clean your gun". "Thank you" Jim replied, stuttering due to the coldness of the sea. "Get those wet clothes off lad" the elderly gentleman said "and I'll see if we have any dry outfits for you" it was when Jim took his shirt off they noticed the bite on his right forearm. "here now lad!" the elderly gentleman said "what's that on your arm?". "erm, I fell through a window" Jim lied. "good!" the elderly gentleman said "because if it was a bite then you'd be right out of that there door!" he pointed to the door behind Jim. "Heidi!" the old man barked "is that broth ready carirad?" Heidi poked her head from round the corner in the kitchen and said "not long now granddad!". Granddad laughed then turned to Jim, "so where have you come from lad? You don't sound like you're from here if you don't mind my saying so?". "Oh not at all!" Jim said "it's been a while since I've had decent conversation with anyone; I'm from Wrexham in North Wales".

"Really?" granddad said, "how've you managed to get down here then?" Jim got changed into the dry clothing that Heidi had just placed in front of him. Once he was fully dressed, Jim sat down by the log fire in front of granddad and told his story.

"It was roughly a week ago when all this stuff started happening, I was home alone like I normally am during the week, my mother and father were at work and my brother was in college, the garden gate closed with a thud which started the family dog barking. I told her to be quiet then went to investigate the noise, there was someone I didn't know in the garden so I went outside to see who they were and needless to say they didn't look like anyone I'd seen before. Suddenly they lurched for me and I knocked them away, as they fell to the ground they started chomping at the air which I found quite strange. By this time the dog was outside with us and as soon as the stranger saw her he lurched for her and bit into her neck. That was the final straw for me so I pushed him off our property then rang for the police. The line was busy so I tried again a few minutes later, still busy. I looked out my window and several people who looked similar to our stranger were gathering in the street. I went to check on my dog, her torso wasn't moving to indicate breathing, she was dead. I began to weep but suddenly her head rose off the floor and she looked at me and began to growl. She leapt up at me chomping air and I realised that whatever had happened to the people outside was now happening to my dog. I didn't know what to do, my head was swimming with possible scenarios, something in the water? A foul bit of beef? I was all over the place. My mind turned to my parents; did they know what was happening? Were they safe? I had to find out. I grabbed the keys to the garage and went outside. The mass of weird people had grown to about fifteen people at my last count. I went into the garage and found a spade that I could use for protection. I fought my way through the throngs of what I now knew to be zombies. I had to get to my friends house in new broughton, he had weapons in his attic, yes, good old Wayne will know what to do! He also had a car that we can go to get my parents in, if it works that is. When I got to Wayne's I knocked loudly on the door. "Piss off!" a voice from the front bedroom window called. "Wayne it's me Jim!" I called back. "Ok I'm on my way down now!" he replied. When he opened the door he took a quick look up and down the street then let me in. We went straight up to his room and assessed the situation. Sitting on his bed was his girlfriend Nicole and my girlfriend Katie, she had come there looking for me when the weird shit started happening where she lived. She had walked there just as I had but she had to out run the zombies as she had no weapons to defend herself with so when Wayne gave me the smith and western I gave her my spade. We began assessing the situation by going on the internet to see if it was all a localised thing. It wasn't. Brutal murders happening all over the world, America, Japan, Russia. We decided we would wait at Wayne's until it all blew over and, in need of supplies, we would only venture out to the newsagents if the place looked safe. I looked out of Wayne's bedroom window, there were a few zombies in the street just milling around not really doing anything in particular. "The front street is off limits" I said to the gang "we may have to take the back alley". So we waited until sunrise to venture out round the back alley taking precaution not to speak loudly as it would attract attention. The journey to the newsagents was extremely eventful, a few zombies in the Chinese take-away having a 'meal' (we couldn't see what was really happening as all the windows were covered in blood and offal). The door to the newsagents was open and the stench of rotting bodies filled our nostrils straight away and every one of us retched. It was lucky that we brought our guns with us as we felt somehow safer holding them, as if safety was just an aim and click away. Wayne and Nicole waited outside while Katie and I went inside to find food and drink. I was in the food section when I heard Katie give a blood curdling scream which was followed by a gurgling moan from a voice I didn't recognise. I ran in the direction of the noise and found this short stocky guy bent over Katie's body eating her. I put the barrel of the gun point blank to the back of the zombies head and pulled the trigger. Gore splattered everywhere and when I shoved the body off Katie I found that she was dead. Suddenly, before I had time to cry, she coughed up blood and her eyes sprung open in a violent, angry way so I had to aim and pull the trigger. The bullet hit her straight between her eyes and she was at peace. I stumbled out the newsagents covered in blood and Wayne and Nicole jumped out of their skin and aimed their weapons at me. I had to scream at them that I was human and that I hadn't been bitten but that Katie was dead. Then we heard moaning and smelled an awful stench on the breeze. The door to the Chinese take-away sprung open and five zombies came out leaving the ruined corpses of the manager of the establishment and his family. Wayne, Nicole and I ran for Wayne's house but as we reached the back alley the zombies from the front street met us so, using the butts of our weapons, we dispatched a few to make way for ourselves. Once we got back to Wayne's we looked out his bedroom window to see his car but the zombies had wreaked it. We decided that it was too dangerous to stay here any longer and if we were going to go we'd have to walk it. "Where are we gonna go?" I asked. "Dragonfield sports" Wayne said "they have a lot of weapons there".

So we made our way through the hordes of the dead, smashing and shooting through showers of gore. We got to Dragonfield sports 20 minutes later and knocked on the door. A pinging sound happened from the window above followed by a voice saying "fuck off you dead pricks!!!", "But we're alive!" Nicole shouted. "Oh ok then!" the voice replied and there was a buzzing sound as the door opened. Inside, like Wayne said, were dozens of weapons, like a cache or arsenal, there was guns and swords of various shapes and sizes, I was quite impressed. The man at the desk (the origin of the voice and pinging sound which we later learned was a gunshot) inspected our weaponry and nodded in approval. He shoved a sword in each of our hands and said "for close combat only" then he laughed. "I don't think we can stay here" I fretted, "chill out lad" the man said "they can't get to us here". I wanted to believe him but, as I looked out the window, I saw that the streets were filling up with dead people. "We've got to go!!!" I called "we've got to go NOW!!!". We went to the door and counted to 3 then barged our way out, chopping and shooting our way through the flesh eating automatons. We lost track of the man at the miners memorial sculpture as he was going the opposite direction, I hope he's still alive somewhere. We decided to try going to Chester to see if there were any survivors we could tag along with. On the way we dipped into a convenience store for supplies, food, cigarettes etc. We were behind the counter picking out liquor to drink along the way when we heard a noise by the magazine aisle, so we went to check it out. There, in a state of shock, was our friend eddy. "Hey you guys!!!" he said with an element of relief in his voice "where are you load off?". "Just off to Chester" Wayne replied "want to come along?". "I don't know" eddy answered "isn't it a bit far?". "Well we were hoping that there'll be survivors there that we can run with" I said. "Ok I'll come, there's not much here anymore anyway" eddy said. So we went off to Chester, dragging a few baskets and trolleys full of supplies, each taking a swig of liquor as we plodded along the baron roads where life used to dwell in it's 9-5 routine, it seems amazing to me now how quickly everything went from normal to chaos then desolation in a matter of hours. We would've felt safer if at least a few people stayed behind to battle the throngs of undead but not even a small mob presented its existence to us as we made our way out of the town, on our way to the big city in search of people who figured out how to live in these conditions, survival techniques and ultimately how to keep the dead from getting back up again, a vaccine, a reason why this all happened in the first place. We were making our way through Gresford when we came across a cadaver with its offal pulled out of a huge cavity in its torso, Nicole threw up, eddy turned way in disgust and Wayne and I, used to scenes like this as we were avid horror movie fans, just looked on in terror as in this scene there was no TV screen to keep us separate from the event. There was a trail of blood and scraps of insides going from the corpse to the door of a near-by house. Wayne and I ventured inside the house and barely got into the kitchen when we were confronted by a pack of skinless dogs and a humongous man who, brandishing an axe came for us. Wayne dispatched him with a trained shot between the man's eyes with his air rifle. I shot a few of the dogs and Wayne finished them off and, blowing the smoke from the barrel of his rifle, walked away smiling to himself. As we went outside we heard Nicole and eddy scream, the corpse with the cavity in its chest was clawing at Nicole's leg trying to bite her so Wayne ran over and caved its head in with the butt of his rifle. It was then that we heard, and smelled, more of them coming. Suddenly in every window and every door of every house they came piling out, attracted by the gun-shots and screaming. We ran and ran for our lives but stopped a few hundred yards down the road as we ran out of breath and thought we would be safe to walk now we were a considerable distance and the undead weren't that fast so they couldn't catch up to us. It was then we realised that, in the midst of all the drama, we'd dropped our supplies and thus had no food or cigarettes or, more importantly to eddy, liquor. On we walked and, as the sun was setting, everything gave off a sinister vibe as shadows emerged from everyday things like hedges and road signs. The moon hid in the clouds for a while then decided to show its face as we passed Darland high school. Within 7 hours we had reached the out skirts of the city of Chester. It looked more desolate and abandoned than Wrexham but we ventured on in hope of finding at least something that resembled life. As we neared the centre of the city we found sign that life used to be there, shopping carts were turned on their sides, pools of blood congregated round blocked drains and, to all our horror, a severed head lay on its side on a bench. "Maybe this wasn't such a good idea" I suggested. "Yeah! You think?" said Eddy sarcastically. "Now now Eddy" Wayne said "there's no need for that!" we looked in the direction of the clock and saw a huge crowd in the street. It was only when the stench got to us that we realised that they were all undead. We decided that populated areas may not be the best choice of residence at this moment in time. So, as Wayne was the only driver in the group, we went looking for a car we could use. We found one parked by where the old cinema used to be so Wayne went to work hot-wiring it. The stench began to get more rank as hordes of the undead came closer. "C'mon

Wayne!!" pleaded Nicole "they're getting closer!!". "Alright alright!" snapped Wayne and with only seconds to spare the car started. Unfortunately Eddy was bitten on his left shoulder as we all clambered into the car. We sped off with me firing a couple of shots in their direction. "We have to take Eddy to the hospital!!" cried Nicole. We decided it was a good idea so we went as fast as the car could go to the countess of Chester hospital. I had ulterior motives to go there as my mother worked in the pharmaceutical section of the hospital and I wanted to know if she was alright or alive at least. When we got there it was deserted so we thought it was safe to carry the ever faster paling Eddy out of the car and to accident and emergency. He was wailing his head off as we tried to move him too quickly but at this point we didn't know how good the undead's hearing was. I asked the group to go on without me as I had to see if my mother was around so I made my way round to Martindale house where my mother worked. I saw her car in the car park and my heart leapt in my throat, on making my way round to the entrance of Martindale house I saw a pool of blood and prayed that it wasn't my mother's. The first door was hanging off its hinges, its windows smashed and also with splatters of blood on them. Whatever happened here wasn't pretty. I got through the first door easy but had to smash the window of the second door with the butt of my rifle in order to unlock the door from the other side. I called out in hope that someone was alive to hear me, but at first had no reply then as I called out a second time I heard someone calling from the tea room. "Mum!!" I said under my breath as I knew that voice from anywhere. I ran towards the tea room but as I got closer to it I realised my mother was trapped in there by three zombies. In order to get to her I dispatched them without a moment's thought as to the likelihood of attracting more of them. I just wanted to get to my mother and know that she's safe, to hell with my own safety. I knocked on the door to the tea room and called out to my mother that it was safe. Then came the sound of clicking as my mother unlocked the makeshift locks on the door. "Oh mum!!" I said as I wrapped my arms around her and held her tightly, "where's dad?" I asked. "He's still at work" she replied "we need to get to him! I tried his mobile on the phone in here and that's when I got trapped by those things!". "Ok mum" I said "let's go!" And we ran out of the building and bumped into the rest of the group but Eddy was missing. Before I could ask them where he was he came stumbling out of the main building, as white as a bed sheet, with blood all down his top where he must've coughed up blood as he died. "Shit!" I said slowly in disbelief and aimed for his head. Before I could get a clear shot Eddy lurched for Nicole, caught her, then bit into her neck. She let out a blood curdling scream and my mother matched her screams in sympathy. Wayne cried out then blew Eddy's head off. Nicole came crying to Wayne and he held her in his arms weeping. "I'll get my car!" my mother said and ran to her vehicle. Within minutes she was there calling for us to get in. "where are we off to?" Wayne asked. "Broughton" I replied "we need to find my dad".

Heidi came in with three bowls of broth for Granddad, Jim and herself. The gun was nearly clean but Granddad set it down beside his chair so he could eat. "I'm sorry to be a burden" Jim asked "but do you have any bread? So I can dip it in this lovely smelling broth". "I'll just go look now" said Heidi. Now, this Heidi, as you're humble narrator failed to mention before, was an incredibly beautiful little thing with assumingly waist length blonde hair done up in the style of Princess Lea from Star Wars. She came back with a few slices of white bread for Jim and he thanked her with a grateful smile and a wink to which she retorted with a sneaking, playful lick of the lips and devilish grin. Jim only managed a few spoonfuls of the broth before he winced in pain and dropped the bowl on the floor, spilling broth everywhere and smashing the bowl on the mosaic tiles of the floor. "My cooking isn't that bad is it?" asked Heidi in a joking tone. "That cut is a bite isn't it boyo?" Granddad asked to which Jim nodded and convulsed in pain as his insides began to slowly die. "Why did you lie to us?" Heidi asked. "Because I was worried that if I told you the truth you wouldn't have helped me" replied Jim. "You're damn right there lad!!" yelled Granddad "but seeing as I've come to get to know you more I'll let you finish you're story". Jim sat up and nodded gratefully.

It was in the car on the way to Broughton that I asked my mother what happened with the door and her work friends. "we tried barricading the first set of doors but they just ploughed through, biting a few of my friends along the way, back then we didn't realise what happened when you get bitten" my mother broke off her story to give Nicole a worried look as she was rocking back and forth looking as though she was going to faint. When she finally stopped moving Wayne began sobbing and wailing uncontrollably. I turned in my seat to comfort him but I wasn't doing anything helpful it seemed. It was then she coughed up blood and sat upright with a sudden jerk, her eyes wide open and crazed. It was then she grabbed Wayne and bit his chest. He cried out in pain, opened her passenger door and pushed her out into the road where her head went under the wheel of the car. When we got to my father's workplace there was a plane on the runway bound for the Isle of Man with people getting on it. Upon closer inspection we saw that my father was there aswell. My parents ran into each other's arms and I felt a tint of happiness in my heart. "Are you coming James?" my father asked. "No" I replied "I'm going to stay here and look after Wayne, I'll get the next flight" I joked. "I really think you should come with us James" warned my mother. "No I mean it I'm staying" I said and that was that. I held my mother and father in my arms tightly and cried. I wanted to go with them but I felt my duty was here with Wayne. I wasn't about to leave him when he needed me most, as he wouldn't with me if our places were exchanged. I wept like a small child on his first day of school as my parents, weeping also, climbed aboard the plane. My mother sat in a window seat and, with tearful eyes, waved goodbye to me as the plane taxied round the runway. As the plane took off I turned and lifted Wayne onto his feet and held him, one of his arms over my shoulder, as we made our way down the road. Over the next few hours we walked and stopped when ever Wayne felt weary. For some reason the virus took longer to manifest itself in Wayne. Maybe it was something in the air that's naturally weakening it, I don't know. When we got to Wrexham we went from travelling on the road to walking on the railway line, again stopping when Wayne needed a break. A day later we reached Shrewsbury train station where Wayne confessed he could go no further. It looked dead apart from the gate on platform 1 which was nearly bent on its hinges with the undead pushing against it. I turned to Wayne in hope and said "if the undead are still loitering here then there must be at least 1 or 2 people still alive here!" Wayne mumbled something unintelligible as I lifted him back onto his feet. We heard the door to the waiting room burst open and I looked up to see my friend Mark and his fiancée Liz waving us in franticly. When we got into the waiting room Mark took Wayne to a sleeping area while I filled Liz in on our travels and everything that happened to us. When I got to the part of the story about my parents flying away on a plane to safety Liz's face went pale and she looked to the floor. "What is it?" I asked. Liz looked up with tears in her eyes and pointed to the radio in the corner which was still broadcasting from a station in Swansea. "The radio said that a plane bound for the Isle of Man ran out of fuel mid flight and crashed into the ocean". I looked to the floor aswell and almost burst into tears but willed them away. "How did you guys get here?" I asked, changing the subject. "Same as you" Mark said "along the train tracks". The night came in with its

purple curtain and we sat down to eat. BBQ ribs and whiskey. It amazed
me how I could still eat after everything I'd witnessed but I had not eaten
since this whole damn thing began and I'd walked many miles carrying my
friend and I was starving. "Where did you get this beautiful feast?" I asked,
enjoying my meal. "We looted a supermarket!" Mark laughed. "Cool!" I
said, almost laughing myself but, considering everything that happened, I
didn't feel like making mirth. After dinner I took vigil by Wayne's bedside,
remembering all the fun we had before all this happened. I figured the
more I make him laugh the less likely he'd fall asleep and never wake up
again. It came to midnight and I felt tired so, looking over at Wayne,
decided to nap awhile. I awoke to screams as it turned out that while I was
napping Wayne had coughed up blood, died and was now eating Mark and
Liz. I grabbed my rifle and drew a bead on Wayne's forehead. I hesitated for
a brief moment but that was all Wayne needed to lurch over to me and bite
my right forearm. I pushed him away and blew his brains out. I dropped
the rifle and sank to my knees and wailed inconsolably, the tears gushing
down my cheeks like waterfalls. I had nothing now but my own pitiful
existence. I stayed knelt there for sometime crying and crying until my eyes
went dry and sore, thinking that I couldn't stay there lest I go mad with my
own company so, taking what little food and drink there was in a rucksack
I found at the security guard station and, picking up the rifle, I hopped
onto the train track again and walked in the general direction of Swansea.
I thought that, if the radio station was still broadcasting, then there must
be at least a few people still alive. Along the way I found an up turned
wooden cart with some blood stains all over it. I approached with caution
whilst loading the rifle ready for anything that might endanger me.
Thankfully there was nothing, the dead that were here might've staggered
to pastures new once the food supply ran out. I decided to check the cart
for anything like food or drink. Instead I found a radio with some batteries
and a copy of junky by William S. Burroughs. "This should help keep my
sanity" I thought out loud. I put the batteries in the radio and scrolled the
tuning plug until I found the station in Swansea. Thankfully they were still
broadcasting so I jumped in the wooden cart and lay back to watch the
stars as dusk was coming in. I lay there for what seemed like days reflecting
on what had happened to me. The friends and family I'd lost. I soon ran
out of whiskey so I rooted through the cart some more and found two
bottles of fine red wine. The radio station DJs were still playing music to
an audience they thought no longer existed which I found to be incredibly

typical of some of the characters I met whilst I lived there for a time. In a haze of drunkenness I sang along to the songs I knew not realising nor at the time caring about the attention I was drawing to myself. All that mattered to me now was getting lost in the music, getting outside myself and away from this bastardised reality that had enveloped itself around me without so much as a warning or care about its effect on the world. On the third day of sitting there I decided I needed a change of scenery and I wanted to meet these DJs in Swansea so I carried on walking along the railroad track every now and then sipping what little wine I had left. Along the road, probably just by Hereford I can't remember, the mixture of wine, whiskey and memories drenched in gore made me violently sick and I threw up the food I had ingested at Shrewsbury. During my time with the radio the DJs became to me as like unrequited best friends as they didn't know I existed but I knew that they were alive and well. That is until I got to Newport and decided to sleep the night. There began a sudden commotion on the air and the signal cut out. Worried, as would anyone who came to know someone in such an intimate and one-sided manner, I gathered my things and sprinted down the railroad tracks for a few yards, grew tired and resigned myself to a brisk walk. I reached Swansea at dawn the following day carefully avoiding Cardiff. I remembered that the DJs said they were transmitting from the old library which is now (or should I say was) the welsh school of architectural glass. I stood at the entrance awhile and wept nostalgically as memories came flooding back to a bright and sunny day in June. I was standing and waiting for my red-haired angel to finish classes for the day. At 3:15pm on the dot she came running down the stone steps and into my arms flooding me with kisses. Just then she and the sun were gone and I was shocked back into the harsh reality. Tentatively I walked up the steps and into the entrance hall of the building. The mechanised doors were hanging off their hinges and the glass was smashed in little diamonds on the tiled floor. Just beyond that, in a pool of blood, lay the body of a heavy-set man with his torso ripped open from his neck to his groin, his ribs sticking out vertically like bony sentinels. Beyond that were the doors to the main part of the library which were also smashed and hanging off the hinges. I cocked my rifle and approached with caution. He didn't move. I walked carefully around him and nearly slipped on my arse in the pool of blood. There was the most offensive odour and a spine-chillingly eerie silence as I entered the main library and was repulsed by the sight I beheld there. The nearest cadaver was one of the DJs sat up-right in his chair, the only thing that still connected his head to his body was his oesophagus. As I entered further I saw the rest of the team in various states of dismemberment and decay, flies and maggots eating what little flesh the undead had left on the bones. I couldn't stay any longer so I decided to turn from this horrific sight and head for the door. I stopped. Lurking around the windows were the silhouettes of various animated cadavers, even our friend with the torn torso. I could hear what was left of his innards slapping as they fell on the tiled floor. I quietly looked around as two more came from around the corner on my right and a further five on my left. Some of them I knew to be my red-haired angel's classmates. I decided to make a run for it and smashed my way past our torso-less friend. Unfortunately I slipped in the blood and offal, dropping my rifle which skidded along the floor. This got the attention of the two on my right and the five on my left. "Ah fuck!" I said under my breath as our friend was clawing at me, trying to eat my legs. I tried manoeuvring myself so he couldn't get a bite in all the while his buddies were drawing closer and closer with every stumbling step. "Shit!" I cried out, caring not for the volume of my voice as I thought things couldn't get any worse. I was wrong. The DJ walked out of the library with his head swaying like a pendulum of a clock. I kicked the man with no torso in the head dazing him a little so as I could get my rifle back. Once in my grip I aimed and squeezed the trigger. There was a crimson waterfall showering over me but I didn't let that stop me. With practiced hand movements I loaded, cocked, aimed and shot until there was nothing there but myself and the headless cadavers littering the corridor. Just then an awful stench enveloped me and there was a smashing sound coming from the entrance. I turned and saw about thirty zombies falling and stumbling through the doors. I felt trapped for a second but remembered there was a back exit so I made for it. When I got there it was already open so I ran through and was met by another ten cadavers in the street reaching for me. I barged my way past them and got a suitable distance and saw outside the main entrance another fifty zombies entering the old library. I remembered my old flat at the top of the hill so I made my way there past hordes of the undead. It was a tiring walk up the steep hill towards my flat, I was amazed that I used to do this every morning and night walking back and to from college. I got to north hill road and saw there was no way of getting to my old flat as there must've been twenty zombies all over the road and in houses. All of them turned and saw me so I ran as fast as I could to Rhondda Street and it was the same there. I began to regret my decision of coming here but it was too late now. I ran to Cwmdonkin Park and the gates were closed so I scaled over them and I collapsed exhausted upon the grass. I heard, and smelt, zombies at the gate but I was safe for the time being. When night came in I got up from the grass and wiped the mud off my trousers. I walked awhile round the park and found a suitable place to sit and try to relax. I remembered I had that book in my bag so I got it out and read a couple of chapters until it got too dark to see the words then I put it away and walked to the second set of gates. They were open but there was nothing dangerous there so I walked and walked all night. Round the marina, through the mall, down Wind Street, around the Dylan Thomas museum, past the cinema which was now in ruins, anywhere there wasn't anything moving and as soon as I saw the faintest bit of movement I was out of there like a scared mouse. As dawn came I sat on the steps by the beach, behind the new library. I saw the sun rising for the first time in what seemed like years and I remembered standing in the kitchen of my flat holding my red-haired angel and watching the sun peek its head from behind the hill, watching the denizens of Swansea leave their houses for work in the morning. Oh the warmth of her embrace, I can still feel it now, the smell of her hair, the touch of her hands on mine. All of this and me thanking her for bringing me down here and her whispering back into my ear. "You're welcome" then the kiss on my cheek. A tear broke from my eye but this pleasantness was interrupted by the familiar stench of the walking dead. I was extremely angry for this interruption of my thoughts as I wanted to be there forever, with her in my arms.

Jim stopped for a moment as a lump came in his throat. He winced with pain from the bite on his arm which was now weeping blood quite profusely. "Is that it?" grandpa said. "Yes" Jim said "for now I guess". Jim took a look around the room and noticed it was night again outside. He winced, then convulsed, then went still. Grandpa picked up the rifle from his side. Jim coughed up blood and a shot rang through the building.

The end

The Last Days of James

I awoke at 6am to a silence you only get in a cemetery on a brisk winters morning, the nurse had just come to check up on me and I think the light from the corridor outside my room was what woke me up. Daylight hours are the only time safe to go outside these days, what with the robots and all, they tend to congregate like a murder of crows outside my window and stare in at me, making false promises of a simpler life, a life without a soul, a life without emotions or humanity, a life where the most difficult decisions you have to make are what colouring you want in your hair, what clothes look good with what, Zach or Steve, Brandi or Susan. But all that was gone now, well, until the sun goes down that is, then they make their dreadful exodus to my window again. I sat up and rubbed my eyes, down the corridor came the dull tones of some insolent news reporter telling how we should cut down on flights because every time we fly we breath in hazardous fumes back drafted from the engine or something, I wasn't really listening. I considered masturbating but, as the hospital had me on close observation, I decided against it. I had slept in my clothes, lest the robots got in and I had to make a speedy exit, so to combat the raging stench of body odour I administered some deodorant and made my way to the lounge of the hendref male ward, llwyn-y-groes psychiatric unit, Wrexham maelor hospital. In the lounge are two nurses I'd quite happily fuck if given the chance, my dick grows hard at the sight of them, and even harder at the thought of them lathered up and ready to nail me like sea biscuit. But of course this is illegal and so can't happen which makes me feel a little down but not too much for me to try and top myself over. I sit and watch the news a little while, what a crock of shit, so I ask if the doors can be opened so I can have a cigarette but the answer is no so I sit and watch the shit on TV again. At 7am they open the doors and I meet the morning and with a sense of desperate relief I stick a Lambert and Butler between my lips and light it. Oh how amazingly orgasmic the fist fag of a morning feels, the way it makes your head spin from the first drag. It was at this moment I woke up fully and realised It was a cruel, grey October morning when the sun hid behind the clouds for fear of being seen, and the trees wailed with the wind, and the leaves were bountiful upon the floor, and the squirrels meekly whimpering as they fight over the nuts in the trees that were wailing like banshees. Then she was beside me, translucent, her hair a brilliant, fiery red, her eyes emerald green, her freckles danced across her face like a ballroom gala.

Her hand stroked my cheek and I wept at the touch of those dainty fingers against my skin, I closed my eyes to stop the tears but they just kept coming.

When I opened them she was gone, leaving me with her slowly dissipating aura.

My cigarette burned my hand, "shit!" I said dropping it.

I went in and made myself some toast and a glass of milk, as I did this Tracy and Kim (who were on night shift) left for home and nurse came in.

"You alright?" she asked in an upbeat way.

"Yeah I guess" was my reply.

"What's up?" she asked "you don't seem your usual chirpy self".

"I just saw Meg again".

"Awww James!" she said, wrapping her huge arms around me "what are we going to do with you?".

At this point my toast popped up and she released me from her embrace.

"You going to be alright to go to college?" she asked.

"yeah I should be fine" I replied, and then I buttered my toast, grabbed my glass of milk and sat at the table to eat.

Once I had finished my satisfying breakfast it was time for me to leave for college (which they allowed me to do as it served as a kind of occupational therapy for me).

On the way I met my beat-nic friend tall cap who resumed our conversation about Jack Kerouac's stories are better than his poetry, to which I replied that he was wrong and that I thought that all Mr Kerouac's writings were good.

At this my friend Noggy walked up and said hi and tried to shake tall cap's hand but tall cap is right handed and Noggy is a leftie.

"I don't trust lefties" said tall cap "they always try to catch you out!".

At this Noggy and I said our farewells to tall cap and continued on our way to college.

At college we sat down on the soft green chairs that line the walls of the lobby to the music department, well, I say lobby, more like a little box room with chairs and several doors leading to other places in the music department.

Soon after, more people began to congregate around this area so Noggy, James Reid (who had just joined us) and I decided it would be a good idea to have a fag outside.

We finished our cigarettes in time for lesson to start, understanding music with Tim Jones, so we made our way to his class where we watched the movie Amadeus; I'd have to say the chick that plays Amadeus's wife in it is hot, I got an instant boner when I saw her, but that's beside the point.

After that lesson I had an itch that I couldn't scratch so I went to fairy spells to see a chick named Roxy and oh boy did she scratch that itch! We must've been at it for hours because I had one hell of a bill afterwards.

After that I met up with my friends in the bowling alley and we drank a lot of shots, must've been 30-40 shots each of red diesel, which is after shock red (cinnamon flavoured liquor), vodka and archers.

During this drinking session Noggy seemed a bit down, so i asked him what was up.

"Ah, it's nothing man, I just wish I could find a girl who'll give me some you know?".

"Yeah man totally" I said, half drunk.

"But what I need is a girl who'll get down and dirty you know what I mean?" he said.

"Well come with me to fairy spells next time I go" I replied.

And then she was there again, with her red hair and her freckles, beckoning me to her, in my mind I go to her and we embrace, and kiss as if it were our last.

I begin to weep as she floats away from me.

"James" a voice says.

"James?" it says again, only clearer.

I find myself being shaken by Noggy and Fiontan.

"Where did you go?" they both say.

"I don't know" I reply, "I just don't know".

After that episode, I decided that it would be best to stop drinking and, as i was already drunk, decided to go back to hospital.

As I went about my journey I bumped into two young girls, vaguely 15 or 16, they were dancing in the library field, "why do you dance?" I asked, "why do you prance?" I implored.

"We dance to save our souls from the kingdom" they answered simultaneously.

"From which kingdom do you flee?" I once again enquired.

"The kingdom of fire and brimstone,
The kingdom of buggeries and rapes,
Where the heat is unbearable,
And virgins are forced naked,
To be defiled on bent knee,
With giant phalluses choking their pleas."

"Is this kingdom known as hell?" I asked.

"In some cultures" they answered.

"What must I do to save my soul from this kingdom?" I asked.

"Dance!" they ordered.

So I danced with them until I could dance no more, my legs began to grow weary, and so I made my way back to hospital.

Once again, along my way, I was stopped, not by a person, but by the realisation that i was in another world.

A world filled with all the vibrancy of a Sunday fair, the now setting sun glowed a brilliant fiery red upon the purple clouds, this amazing glow took on the form of hairs, moving in the breeze, and the setting sun, a face and forehead, I did not see the mouth, but I knew, in my drunken state, that the face was speaking to me, freckles danced upon the nose and cheeks, and the eyes were of emerald green, I knew that face, the face that haunts my dreams night after night, I began to weep, and the cooling breeze warred with my tears, as if to attempt to dry my cheeks and eyes.

But I shook myself out of this with the realisation that the robots would be on their way, and with haste, I made my way back to hospital.

That night was terrible, they plagued me all the way through, mocking my tears and my cries for mercy, and even in the smoke room they still bothered me with their promises and their denials, in an attempt to assimilate me as they did with my beloved, this took me back to that night, the night of her assimilation, the night she joined the ranks of the mentally undead, the night HE came and took her from me.

A handsome stranger strolls into the bar of the dragon hotel in Swansea.

He clocks a succulent, young lady working behind the bar, she had red hair, green eyes and freckles on her face, he knew he could fuck her if he tried hard enough, all he need was an opening and her working behind the bar was just the opening he required

"A brandy and coke please" he said to her in a smooth baritone.

"Coming right up" she said in a weary monotone.

"Long day?" he enquired.

"yeah, I started at 7am" she said, glad that he'd started the conversation, as, even though she hadn't seen him before, she felt strangely attracted to him, more than her poet boyfriend of four years.

She made him the drink and they continued talking as he drank.

"So where you from?" he asked.

"I'm from Stafford originally, then I moved to Wrexham, met my boyfriend and now we live down here" she replied.

"Boyfriend?" he asked, raising one eyebrow "if I were he, I'd be very careful where I'd let you go at this time of night, because, if you don't mind my saying so, you are the most beautiful girl I've ever seen, you don't know who's about to take advantage!"

"Well that's the thing" she said "I don't think he cares anymore, he seems preoccupied with his writing, he's something of a poet you see".

"A poet?" he exclaimed, this hard body was going to take some working on if he wanted to get in her pants tonight, "what kind of stuff does he write?"

"Oh he varies from the classic stuff like Edgar Allen Poe to the more modern, beat-nic stuff like Allen Ginsberg" she replied, noticing that as she was talking, he was licking his lips and looking her up and down with big, brown eyes, this excited her somewhat and her nipples went hard.

She didn't have the normal body of someone the tender age of 19 going on 20, her breasts were large and natural but her stomach didn't protrude, she had amazing hips and an even more amazing arse, she was perfection.

"Oh that's very interesting" he mocked, but she didn't pick up on it until a few moments later when she gave a slight grin and her cheeks went the same colour as her hair.

At this he saw that she was in the net and all he needed to do was play it cool and get her to come up to his room so he can 'seal the deal' as they say.

"You ever had your picture taken?" he asked "professionally I mean".

"No" she replied.

"Would you like to?"

"Sure!"

"Ok meet me in my room in half an hour; my name is Raoul Francois, and what name am I honoured to address thee?" he said in his smooth, sensual baritone.

"Megan" she said quietly, her face now beaming, her heart pounding and her nipples almost pointing through her shirt, her sex had now also began to get profusely wet with every word Raoul uttered.

Who was this Raoul? And why had she agreed to go to his room with him?

She searched his name on the guests list, Raoul Francois, room 486.

Half an hour later she knocked nervously on his door, and when he answered he was naked, holding a professional photographer's camera, Megan considered leaving when she remembered that her boyfriend was at home waiting for her, but, considering the impressive size of Raoul's genitalia and the fact that she was now sopping wet, she decided to enter his room.

In his room, Raoul took a few photographs of Megan as she posed alluringly.

"Right!" he said "take your shirt off".

She slowly, if a little reluctantly, did as instructed and took her shirt off to expose her impressive top figure.

"Well, well, well" he said smiling devilishly "you are impressive!"

"Thank you" she says meekly "I haven't heard someone say that in a long time!"

She lies! Her boyfriend said it to her everyday.

She was wearing red lingerie, a sure sign that she was up for anything.

"Take off your trousers" he ordered "I want to see your full beauty".

She took her trousers off, slowly still but turned it into a tease.

Raoul placed the camera on the bedside table and walked towards her. She couldn't keep her hands off him and it was then they made love.

On the chest of draws, on the bed, in the shower, on the bathroom floor, just a flurry of fucking, rutting, sucking and licking.

By the time the deed was done the night was through and the day was dawning.

Megan knew then that she could never look at her boyfriend the same way again.

I screamed out my pain at this awful memory, how could she? What had I done?

I decided it was time to get my medication to try and get these memories out of my head for a while so I left the smoking room and went to the hub to get them.

10mg of Aripiprizole and 50mg of Sertraline, along with a tablet of Irazipan to help me get to sleep.

Once I had gotten changed into my pyjamas and settled down in bed the tablets had taken effect and I sank into a dreamless sleep.

The robots were gone, Raoul and Megan were gone, just me and the obsidian void that comes with a dreamless sleep.

Again I awoke at 6am and again the two nurses were in the TV room, and again they were watching shit on TV.

Again I wanted to fuck them, again I couldn't and again I didn't let it bother me.

At 7am the doors opened and I went out for my morning smoke, I watched what would be my last sunrise, peaking over the hills with a horizon of purples and reds then noticed something lying on the floor, upon further and cautiously closer inspection; I discovered it was a robot, an injured robot at that.

I approached it with caution, wondering what it was doing out in the open at this time of day.

It spoke as I drew near.

"Heya kid!" it said, gasping for breath "you couldn't get a nurse could you?"

I was wary at first as I didn't know his intentions but I soon realised that if I could get him inside I could UN-assimilate him and bring him back to humankind.

"Sure!" I said.

I got one of the nurses to have a look at him and she came to the conclusion that he was faking it.

Fooled! By a robot!

I was fuming, inconsolable, I couldn't believe I'd let myself get fooled into believing a robot! Let alone talking to one.

At that moment I retired to my room and wrote a song with my guitar.

'Strings' was the outcome.

The angriest song I'd ever written.

It was then I came to the conclusion that the robot had been faking an injury to play possum, to get in the ward at me, to infiltrate my place of sanctity, safety and relief.

They'd found a way of getting in, I needed to flee.

Swansea was the place I needed to be.

So at that moment I left the hospital, and ran to the bank to get some money out, I'd been paid! Hallelujah! Enough money to get down to Swansea!

I drew the money out and fled to the train station.

My only hope of salvation was to enter the heart of the robot's lair and retrieve my long lost love from their clutches, UN-assimilate her or die trying.

It was early morning so I had enough time to get there, the train pulled into the station and I boarded, saying my final farewell to Wrexham.

The train journey was a fairly easy one, there was no-one on the coach I was in save the ticket man and even he didn't come up to me to take my fare.

I passed the racing countryside with its horizon of greens, yellows, blues and browns, vaguely noticing a house or two, but it all just blurred together as the train picked up more speed.

The train stopped at Newport for the change and I quickly rang my contacts on the inside little miss sunshine and her sister pineapple from a payphone, they agreed to meet me at the local pizza parlour so we can talk.

The instant I hung up I started to get a dark cloud hanging above me, "don't go!" this dark cloud said.

"I have to" said I, seemingly talking to myself.

Half an hour later the train bound for Swansea turned up, I was reluctant to get on but I pondered to myself 'if I don't get on this train I never will' so I got on and found a seat away from everybody.

The ticket man came as soon as we left the station.

"Tickets please" he said rather monotonously.

"Can I have a return to Swansea please?" I enquired.

"Where from?" he asked.

"Wrexham please".

"Ok that's £40.60" he said.

I payed my money and he left me alone after giving me my tickets.

All along that quiet journey I thought of what the dark cloud had told me and I came to the conclusion that I must do this in order to get my long lost love Megan back or at least get some closure.

I stood by the door as we pulled into Swansea train station, all around I noticed robots marching to the beat of their electronic music, the train screeches to a halt as if some sort of animal was caught under its wheels, I open the door and take a step outside, I feel a rush of anxiety flow over me like a tsunami, 'keep your cool' I thought, turning it into a mantra 'you can do this, just walk in there and get her back'.

Just outside the station, little miss sunshine and pineapple were waiting for me.

"I'm feeling a little nervous" I warned them "can you hold my hand or something?"

"Sure" little miss sunshine said, and she took my hand in hers.

Oh that hand felt so warm and comforting, I could tell she hadn't been assimilated yet.

We went to the pizza parlour but on the way we were forced to pass the epicentre of the robot's lair, the Swansea school of architectural glass, and my blood ran cold.

Many times I waited outside that building for my love to end her lessons for the day, all the while the robots were conspiring against me, whispering in her ear "leave him, join us, we will make life easier for you".

Outside the building stood two of the conspirators, like great, big, mechanical monoliths they seemed to tower over us, and glare judgementally at us as we made our way past them, their grey skin beginning to fray as their circuitry protruded through, forcing its way out into the open to breath, their designer clothing, however, remained untouched.

When we were past them, I got a chill down my spine as I realised they were sending me daggers with their LED eyes, the lasers piercing my mind in search for bait.

'Get out' I thought 'you're not welcome here'.

When we rounded the corner the feeling passed and I was safe again.

In the pizza parlour we ate and we talked and we reminisced of old times, like when we got drunk in the biker bar off wine street on this amazing drink I'd made up called the 'purple Johnny' which consisted of after shock red and WKD blue.

"Oh!" said pineapple nostalgically "those were the days, THOSE WERE THE DAYS!!!"

"Yeah!" little miss sunshine chimed "damn!"

"Well I can't lie to you guys" I said "I miss them! I miss them a hell of a lot!"

"Can't we repeat them?" asked little miss sunshine.

"Nah!" said I "I've got a mission to do today".

"Which is . . . ?" asked pineapple.

"I'm going to try and get Megan back, I don't know how, but I'm going to try!" I explained.

Anyway, we'd finished our respective meals and I bid them a fond farewell and left my share of the bill on the table.

As I made my way down the streets towards the robot's lair the dark cloud returned, "Go home" it said "this will serve you no good!"

I took a long hard thought about it, wondering whether or not to follow the dark cloud or continue with my mission.

I decided, after careful consideration, that I must get some Dutch courage before doing this and I made my way to the fabled biker bar, my cheers, where everyone knows my name.

I reached the biker bar in what seemed like no time at all, not even noticing the dragon hotel, the scene of my love's assimilation by Raoul, the bastard.

When I got there it was closed.

"I'm going to have to do this sober" I said to myself.

So I turned around and walked back in the direction of the station.

"Go home" the dark cloud had returned "this will serve you no good!"

I ignored the dark cloud's warning and carried on my way.

When I reached the door of the robot's lair I hesitated, there was no-one here keeping guard, then I heard why.

There was a faint sound of chanting coming from within, I opened the door and the chanting became louder, there was a security door that I had to get through, I didn't know the code for it so I exited the building and sat outside for a smoke.

Whilst I was smoking I remembered that there was a fire exit at the back which is almost always left open.

So I made my way round the back to see if it was.

It was.

I breathed a sigh of relief and finished my cigarette.

I entered the fire exit and, as I did so, the chanting was louder and it echoed down the hallways, I didn't exactly know what they were saying but I could make some words out.

Robotic and marriage.

I snuck down the corridor, making sure my boots didn't click on the ceramic tiling that made up the floor.

I came to the door of the room where the chanting was coming from and looked through the window.

There was a congregation just standing and chanting this seemingly in-audible chant, but there in the midst of this congregation, in all her finery, was my long lost beloved Megan standing in the centre of the room, and beside her stood Raoul.

Beyond them was a huge computer, whirring and buzzing away.

Just then, the door gave way and I fell through it and onto the floor, the chanting stopped abruptly, I could feel their eyes looking down their noses at me, I struggled to look up and when I did I could see Megan and Raoul walking towards me.

As she came closer, I realised that Megan had turned from an object of great, natural beauty into something hideous, synthetic.

She'd lost weight and looked emaciated, her eyes had sunken into her now protruding cheek bones and her wrists were so slight, it brought a tear to my eye to see what they'd done to her.

"What do you want?" she said, coldly.

"I want you back!"

"No chance mate!" laughed Raoul "she's mine now; I made sure of that, something, I hear, you weren't able to do because you were too drunk half the time!"

All the robots laughed, in unison, their cold monotonous laughter.

"I don't want you, you made my life hell, coming home at all hours drunk out of your mind!" said Megan once again, coldly.

"I was breaking on through to the other side, getting inspiration so that I could write great poetry so that I could get it published so we could have a nice house somewhere in the country and raise a family together!" I pleaded.

"That's not going to happen now she's mine is it mate?" chuckled Raoul and the congregation chuckled along with him.

"I'm not your mate you bastard!" I said "I'm far from your mate!"

At this I stood up and said "Megan please! I implore you, come back to me!"

"Just get out, you little piece of filth!" was her reply.

I began to weep and everyone instantly began laughing, even Megan.

This object of former beauty had become fully assimilated and all was lost, I was inconsolable, tears ran down my cheeks as I was frozen by the steely, mechanised laughter that began to envelope me completely.

I turned and fled but the robots had blocked my only means of escape, they laughed and laughed as I wept uncontrollably, trying to fight my way past them, but alas they would not relent in their mocking or concede in their barrier against the door.

"Awww! Crying to mummy?" one of them said, and then let out an ice cold cackle.

There was a male robot standing directly in front of the door, so I tried to push past him, he would not relent, he just stood there and laughed, so I punched him to the floor and ran through the door as quick as a gazelle fleeing from a hungry leopard.

When I reached the street, I turned right and ran down to the train station, behind me were robots, including the one I had hit, chasing me and screaming "get him!" and "someone call the police!", up ahead were little miss sunshine and pineapple, so, in a fit of hysterics, I told them everything.

By the time I'd finished they were looking at me as if I were mad, then I noticed the grey skin, the LED laser eyes and the circuitry under their skin.

All was lost, I felt totally helpless and I ran again, away from everything and everybody, to the only place I knew was safe, Cwmdonkin Park.

There I wept for a while, under the tree where only months beforehand, Megan and I had buried our beloved pet mouse Cream.

And then for one final time, she was beside me, translucent as always.

She handed be a hammer and nail, and then pointed to my belt and then the branch which hung above us, I knew what I had to do.

I climbed the tree to the first branch, took my belt off and made a makeshift noose then hammered it into the branch.

I slipped it over my head.

Weeping, I said my last goodbyes to a world that never understood me, a world where it's a crime just to be who you are, a world that's on its way to hell.

The sun was beginning to set by this time, and I sat and watched it a while, the sky was a clear, brilliant orange and red, and at the foot of the tree a murder of crows came to take my soul to peace, cawing their greetings to me.

I leaped off the branch and began to choke, my legs kicking furiously in a galloping motion and my eyes glazed over, it was then all went black and I knew . . . . I was finally free.

The end.

Salvia Trip

In a Cadillac with friends,
Everyone has their garden,
Mine of pure excess,
Drink, you can't die,
Drop acid, you can't die,
Lay with anyone you like, you can't die,
I see the garden at the side of the road,
Better lighten the load,
I jump out but don't land,
I blow a cloud, handful of sand,
Moon dust on my face,
I'm in outer space,
Safe,
Happy,
Feeling nice,
Whole,
The mother figure,
The supplier,
Never be a liar,
Always be there for us,
Never leave us,
Always dependant on him,
My friends are planets,
We breath in a sigh,
We are flying high,
Revelations in the summer breeze,
Past knowledge proved false,
The sun makes the sand look like gold,
The sand feels light underneath me,
And I get a tingle all over my body,
Changes in scenery,

The moon is big in the sky,
I fall backwards and through the floor,
Drowning in sand like water,
Black all around except for the moon,
The dish is having an affair with the fork,
The spoon is envious,
I'm concussed,
Pure genius comes in perceptive cleansing,
Have you heard history?
Milking a former glory,
I'm happy and know no bounds,
On the road with friends,
Night parties on the beach,
"man! Don't smoke it to the end!"
The sea breeze makes me stutter,
The drink makes me slur,
Your heart melts like warm butter,
Heartache there is no cure,
She smiles and beckons me,
Kisses and fellates me,
She tells me a story,
And her eyes turn into cold rainbows,
Her mouth,
A river of words flowing into my ears at full torrent,
Give up life for lent,
If you fail,
You sin,
What will you leave for your kin?
A joke book?
A mattress?
The address for the local temptress?
Or maybe a pocket watch from Peru,
That doesn't work to mess up life for you,
Or maybe a bottle of whiskey to sink into.

The Gentle Poet

The gentle poet stands on the mound,
Waiting for all the freaks to gather round,
Feet held firmly on the ground,
He stood like the accused at the trial of his life,
His humdrum life,
Accompanied by his weeping wife,
Who was by his side knelt,
Dealing a card she was dealt,
Did her no harm,
'cept the scars on her arm,
On his other side stood his friends,
Who were there to the end,
Or til it got too much for them,
Now the freaks begin to gather,
Over the hill they stagger,
Like a rolling wave of part-time minions,
Hoping for something new,
To awaken them,
Like a drop of morning dew,
Upon their media made blind-folds,
The freaks reach the foot of the mound,
Desisted movement, desisted sound,
The gentle poet looks to the heavens,
Now rumbling and black with storm clouds,
Proclaiming to the crowds,
"No!"
T'was not the crowds that put him off,
But the threat of becoming a trough,
For these pigs,
These snorting pigs,
Raising his voice over the coming thunder,

Carefully so as not to blunder,
"T'is not the weather,
To be sitting amongst the heather,
Again I say to you,
You small listening few,
NO!"
At this he turned away,
And faced a bright new day,
No loyal friends,
No weeping wife,
No freaks,
Just his own company,
And a bottle of California red,
The sun is in the gutter,
The desecration of something pure,
Your heart melts like warm butter,
Heartache there is no cure,
Bent and blue and gray and old,
Begging for a break,
Away from the cold,
The gentle poet sips his wine,
Yearning to see,
The path of luxury,
Long haired, bearded
He makes his way across a sandy ocean,
Swansea beach is where he's at now,
Prowling at night like a cat, wow!
Look at him go,
Watch him flow,
Watch him go with the flow,
Mellow flow of life,
Keep watching even though,
He's getting drunk and you're learning to sew,
Yearning to sew,
A great big jumper,
Run along like thumper,
"Seldom sees the blinking eye,
The beauty of a summer morning,

Amidst the hills of heather,
A new day is dawning"
He writes and recites,
In a stupor, be of drink or,
Of sleeping pills, which is lore,
T'is not the gentle poet that knoweth more,
But the paramedics rapping on his chamber door,
"Let us enter,
Let us enter!"
They implore,
Once again rapping on his chamber door,
"Nay, I say!" rambles the gentle poet,
All bent and blue and grey and old,
"Get thee from my door, get thee away from my door!"
Nevermore,
Forevermore,
Rapping on his chamber door,
Comes the persons of his life,
His weeping wife,
His loyal friends,
His freaks,
Coming to his chamber door,
"Let me be" he cries "let me be!" he screams,
As he falls asleep forever,
And dreams,
Dreams of himself,
Of within himself,
You better run,
Because Mr. Hyde has come out,
For fun,
Til the rising sun,
The gentle poet bids adieu,
It has come full tilt,
The drink has come full tilt,
Fucking whores up to the hilt,
Or maybe some poor old schmo,
Wearing a kilt,
The scarlet dripping from defiled ass,

Sitting, smoking some prime grass,
Talking of life experiences,
With his brothers of the bottle,
Singing song of wine, women and times of old,
Of rolling hills of emerald green,
Of lost lovers,
Of lovers lost,
Let me set the scene,
Dirty nature,
The nurse asks
"We're losing him, what do we do?"
The place is vibrating,
Like a rampant rabbit on full whack,
The gentle poet slips into dream,
Seldom sees the thinking eye,
Seldom sees the eye that blinks,
What a fellow poet truly thinks,
And dreams,
He's falling apart at the seams,
Out of this state he screams,
By his side is a bowl of jelly and ice cream,
Held by his brothers of the bottle,
Talking about living life full throttle,
At the end of the day,
All a poet has is his bottle,
A bottle of rum,
A bottle of wine,
Whatever it takes,
To see the beauty of thine,
Brothers of the bottle,
Part-time minions,
He proclaims to thee,
"Nevermore, nevermore!"
Watch him go,
Look at him flow,
Flow of whiskey,
He has the key,
To a great life,

With his wife,
Who weeps,
Weeps tears of woe,
With no way of letting go,
Weary of this scene,
He slips into dream,
He philosophises,
"Only a true poet lives a life of woe,
Only a true poet never lets go",
He dreams of his weeping wife,
And him walking the moors and streets,
Of Glaisdale,
He dreams of his ostricisation at Yale,
Simply because he wasn't 'cool',
Whatever that is,
He dreams of testing the bounds of reality,
Through means of immorality,
Meeting his brothers of the bottle,
Living life full throttle,
He dreams of his funeral,
They lay him low,
Sink him in the snow,
Premature casualty,
Of hedonism,
Pre-Madonna,
They miss him when he's gone,
Detest him when he's around,
Friends throw smokes for the road,
Family throw roses,
A victim of fickleness,
When he was unknown,
Before fame,
He was disliked,
But as soon as he was in the spotlight,
"We knew him, he was cool!"
Lies!
Laying in his casket,
His cowboy boots sticking out,

He dreams of the dirt falling heavily on the casket lid,
RAT!
TAT!
TAT!
You know what that is?
That's the devil knocking on that casket lid of his,
Blinding dark,
Searing heat,
He dreams of scorning teachers,
Shame preachers,
Preachers of shame,
Because no one gets treated the same,
Not even the special people,
The teacher preacher pets,
Grossly paid sadists,
Always stuck with the wrong person for the job,
He's told that his dream,
Is the vengeance of god,
To show all his flaws,
Just for a downer,
To be the subject of ridicule,
For all the frowners,
The kingdom of fire and brimstone,
The kingdom of buggeries and rapes,
Where the heat is unbearable,
And virgins are forced naked,
To be defiled on bent knee,
Giant phalluses choking their pleas,
The big bully says,
"You're cruising for a bruising",
The gentle poet cries in shame,
As the other children dance around his puddle,
Chanting "he's pissed in the playground, he's pissed in the playground!"
Another child says "I celebrated your brother's death!"
Frightening angry father,
Distant mother,
French kissing brother,
Who makes the gentle poet watch him as he pisses,

Or shits,
Raped by his best friend,
Left by his weeping wife,
At the trial of his life,
His humdrum shitty life,
A prayer for the unborn,
Who are yet to be,
Scorned, bullied, raped, abused,
Left for dead,
Life's better off living in your head,
This is the way,
Step inside,
The mind and life of a gentle poet,
Searching forever on this road,
The gentle poet seeks,
The long lost love of his life,
His weeping wife,
Lost,
Forever,
Never,
Ever,
Ever roaming this road,
Of creaking doors,
And damp moss growing in the corners of the room,
Covering everything in dark mould,
He sits at the edge of the double bed,
Writing out what's in his head,
Horrible scenes,
Of rape,
Of torture,
Of the Shetland pony mum and dad bought ya,
All he wants is some closure,
To hear it from the horse's mouth,
But this horse's mouth is shut firm,
And says no words,
Apart from what the robots tell it to say,
Wise men teething,
And seething,

Following yonder star,
Or so is said,
Indoctrination of the lovers lost,
Sanity is the cost,
Not of the past loves,
But of the lone doves,
The gentle poet asks himself,
"Why do they leave you when you need them most?"
Whom is the host?
Holy ghost?
A slice of toast?
Each scar on his arm,
Represents a wrong doing,
Unto himself,
To himself,
He's just another broken toy on the shelf,
Gathering dust,
Whilst his heart's former lover,
Or owner,
Is in lust,
In must,
Oh! How awful this feeling,
It's sending the mind reeling,
Out of control,
Out of day,
And it is night-time,
The robots are in hiding,
The gentle poet is safe to wander,
This road,
He drops his empty bottle of wine,
Better lighten the load,
His heart is thine,
Weeping wife,
Do as thy see fit!
"i'm not afraid" he sings,
"to admit i adore you!"
Once upon a time,
'neath trees of lemon,

And lime,
There sat two lovers,
Entwined,
Drinking their wine,
In silence,
In awe of Mother Nature,
In all its glory,
T'is the beginning of this story,
That we must look to see,
The path of luxury,
His weeping wife is smiling,
Long before she began to weep,
Taking the gentle poet's soul,
To keep,
Long before his muse,
Long before his use,
Of the bottle,
And of despair,
Long before his weeping wife found another,
That bastard, her lover,
The cause of the flow of whiskey and wine,
It was him,
HIM!
He who made the gentle poet look a drunken fool,
Standing in his own pool,
Of past experiences,
Its getting deeper and deeper,
He's drowning,
Help him! Help him!
Take his outstretched hand,
This isn't what he'd planned,
Standing there,
Smoking duty paid cigarettes,
Waiting for fairy spells to open,
He thinks back to his daughter,
And the values he could have taught her,
He prays to take back the abortion,
He prays for some sort of redemption,

It sure makes a long time man feel bad,
Thinking back to what he could've had,
Then it hits him,
BAM!
Like a freight-train,
Reality's a bitch,
Stone cold buttercup,
Oh our poor, grief stricken, gentle poet!
May he rest in peace,
May he forever rest in peace,
May he find peace in the kingdom,
May his soul glide gently among the doves,
In the sky,
In the beholder's eye,
Where he can while away his time,
Writing the beauty all around him,
Like a melancholic social commentator,
Displaying a love impossible to hide,
Doing anything to be by your side.

The Pain of Love

Remember the times when we laughed,
At the world that scorned and scoffed,
All we did and all we said,
Our dreamboat sank,
In the ocean of the world's judgement,
The robots took you from me,
Ripped you from my cradling arms,
My little shining light of red hair,
Leaving me a hollow shell of a man,
Without remorse or feeling,
They took the only thing,
Worthwhile in my shallow life,
All I knew was you,
All I had was you,
Now you're gone,
I know nothing,
But void,
Endless void,
Give me the death you like to tease,
It would take me with ease,
You said forever,
I should have known,
You meant never,
As I lay here dying in your arms,
The pain of love is prevalent,
In all its glory,
And I am comforted by my last breath.

A gunshot in Christland

A gunshot in Christland,
Blood washes away the sacred sand,
Death is the only sound,
Bodies litter the Christian ground,
See the 6 foot hole in the ground,
Be the first to jump in,
Be the first to repent sin,
Be the first to 'take Christ as your saviour',
Let him lead you,
Under false pretences of paradise,
To the hole again,
The F.A.Q is always "When? When? When?",
Don't be coy,
Just enjoy,
What you have at the moment,
Before you plunge into the hole again,
Look into the sky,
Look Christ in the eye,
He's laughing,
Up there,
In his paradise of serenity,
Where everything goes as sweet as a birdsong,
"What about earth?" one angel asks,
"Fuck them" Christ replies.

Big green fly

Rate these scars,
Rate these scars,
Then make yours better than all of ours,
Self proclaimed victims and their arrogance,
Beat me half to death with their ignorance,
You're a whining loser,
The beggar and the chooser,
You depend upon your loved ones,
To pay your way,
Get the fuck off your high horse,
Get ready to feel the force,
Of life in the great wide world.
Bright new day

Every time I see the sunrise,

I think of you,
And your amazing eyes,
It fills me with glee,
Especially that smile,
We flock upon sun kissed sands,
You've got me eating,
Right out of your hands,
You can call me crazy,
And I'll call you by your name,
In blessed succour,
I greet the dawn,
My tears fall,
But not from despair,
But from the beauty of it all.

Discarded

I can see why you picked him,
He's ten times what I could be,
Ten times what I could ever be,
Why would Ophelia want me?
When she could have her pick of the gods,
Living life in Iago's shoes,
Skin clinging to my frame,
I saw the impatient look,
Upon your angelic, sweet face,
When you met me under the tree,
Under the bouncing willow bows,
Under the showering autumn leaves,
Your smile,
Your red hair,
Oh god!
It's more than I can bare,
And he's laughing,
Standing there,
Oh god!
It's more than I can bare,
Drowning in scarlet release,
Putting life back together,
Piece by piece,
Then you come along,
Weeping your lovely song,
And smash my vase.

I love you (until death do us part)

I love you,
You are my Aphrodite,
Together we shy away,
From the light,
I love you and you own my heart,
And I'll love you until death do us part,
Nothing can stop me,
And I'll love you until death do us part,
In the heaven of your arms,
You cure my pain and suffering,
Don't be afraid to sing your song,
Always know,
Even in death,
I'm listening.

Morning Insomnia

Somewhere between wake and sleep,
Terrible time I'm forced to keep,
The wee-small hours,
My eyes ache,
Cemetery silence,
No one's awake,
Not even the birds,
I've not yet seen one fly,
The sun is not yet in the sky,
Waiting for dawn,
On a condinsated lawn,
Locked out your house,
Curled up like a mouse,
Just writing what you're reading,
Before my morning feeding,
The sun comes now,
With her warm glow,
Just a short note before I go
It's been a pleasure killing you,
But the police are coming,
I'll just stroll away casually,
A happy tune I'm humming.

Peeping Tom

I espied her through the petals,
As she bathed in the clearing,
Caressing my features with erotic ferocity,
A look of maniacal pleasure,
Spread across my face,
Out in the dark,
Where no one saw them,
Primeval instinct,
Takes over logical mind,
The snake was hard and weeping,
The temple gates,
Wide open and soaking,
Dare I take Romeo's climb?
To see the naked beauty of thine,
In the sleeping hours,
You are still,
Empty spaces,
That we fill,
So serene,
To see you breathing,
Inside you are rotten and seething,
Your heart already won,
I'm weeping with unrequited passion,
As thick as the window that separates us,
I had one of my turns today,
So just keep away,
I want to kill you,
I want to fuck you,
I want to cook you,
I want to eat you,
I followed you home,

Right to your door,
I climbed your drainpipe,
I saw you kiss him,
Now you're in my house,
A dirty old shack of a house,
You're not going anywhere now,
You are mine forever,
You're tied to my bed,
Fragile as a doll,
Oh god,
You've just shit yourself,
Your face is broken,
So goddamn decayed,
Blood-stained crowbar,
In my trembling hand,
It's enough to drive a man to kill,
If I can't have you,
No one will,
LOVE!
Cruelly,
She keeps me,
Always near to her heart,
In my mind she dances naked,
T'is her art,
Under the dark and ancient oak,
I take her photograph,
My hopes,
She will dash,
I'd better turn off the flash,
I cut myself for your love,
Write you a poem with my blood,
I'll kill the man you are with,
Sing you a song outside your window,
Taking Romeo's climb,
Through your window I creep,
Over to your bed,
Your lamp is on,
I recite Shakespeare,

"I put out the light,
Then I put out the light",
You suddenly did awake,
Your eyes filled with fear,
I smother you with your pillow,
And retreat towards your window,
I run out towards the night,
Clasping your life's light.

She has Monkies (I wonder why)

I jump out the bath,
Walk down the garden path,
To see the leaves of autumn,
Fly up into the green sky,
And I wonder why,
I see gnomes,
Who don't have homes,
I laugh out loud,
See the mirth in my eye,
And I wonder why,
She has Monkies,
Who are secret junkies,
See the needles on the bathroom floor?
They claw for more,
I wonder why,
Take a hit from the lung,
Before you're hung,
Make sure you're beaten,
Before you've eaten,
Being defiled makes your hair go wild,
And I wonder why,
Test drive the bike,
Any colour that you like,
Make sure you count the drinks you spike,
I'm flying with Lucy and her diamonds in the sky,
And I wonder why,
WHAM!

Fly down the garden path,
To the suddy safety of my bath,
Mr Spider is on the wall,
Looking bewildered,
And I wonder why.

Society

Women weekly exploration,
Exploiting secrecies,
Like an explicit striptease,
Who does this please?
The average Joe?
Or the bitter foe?
Stress heads go with the flow,
Because you reap what you sow.

The hypocrisy of love

Go then . . . .
Go then fall in love with them,
Smile now during my requiem,
Go see the priest after the show,
In the confessional booth,
Where no one will know,
Go gently now,
Don't choke,
In that box of hypocrisy and oak,
As Jehovah wins,
The right to all your sins,
You sprout your wings of white feather,
And scarlet leather,
At the wake,
The saddening wake,
He tastes your lake,
Your lustful lake,
The celibate clergy is a fake,
He's older,
And colder,
And hence,
Has more experience,
Your companions,
His accomplishments,
Their promiscuous tales,
Arouse your curiosity,
Could he fill you,
With shameless glee?

His eyes and smile do invite,
You must feel his sexual might,
Pressure from your peers,
Floats like waves,
Into your ears.

The poppy burns black

Atop a mountain slope,
I sit alone,
Without hope,
I hear a sobbing sound,
From deep within the ground,
A whisper tells me to go,
It begins to snow,
I look up into the sky,
And a snowflake falls into my eye,
I clear my eyes and see,
A burning tree,
At the slope's bottom,
It's not yet autumn,
The inferno spreads like a rash,
These snowflakes are ASH!!!

The shattering of life

You are dammed,
To your immorality,
The limit of your sleep,
Exceeds my reality,
The blood is the life,
When lanced by a knife,
In your eyes,
I see death,
In mine ears,
Your last breath,
I take a gasp,
Your throat I will grasp,
Hatred I will not lack,
When your eyes roll back,
Now I live,
Happily ever after,
No more will my sadness,
Be a chorus of your laughter,
T''is a dream of mine,
To drink your flowing wine,
As you lay dying,
Upon a shrine.